D1419140

Explaining
The Cross

Dr Bob Gordon

Sovereign World

Scripture quotations are from the Holy Bible, New International Version,
© Copyright 1973, 1978 International Bible Society.
Published by Hodder & Stoughton, unless otherwise stated.

NKJV—New King James Version © Copyright 1983 Thomas Nelson Inc.,
Box 141000, Nashville, TN 37214, U.S.A.

Authorised King James Version

ISBN: 1-85240-062-5

Production & Printing in England for
SOVEREIGN WORLD LIMITED
P.O. Box 17, Chichester, West Sussex PO20 6YB
by Nuprint Ltd, Station Road, Harpenden, Herts AL5 4SE.

Contents

1

Behold The Lamb

The centre of the Bible is Calvary! Everything before leads up to it and everything after leads from it. What happened on the Cross of Calvary is for God, the most important event since the creation of the world, and it will remain the most important event for ever. The Bible declares:

> *Now, once at the end of the ages, He has appeared to put away sin by the sacrifice of Himself.*
> (Hebrews 9:26, NKJV)

The Christian faith is unique, not because it recognises man's problem and need, but because it also recognises that man cannot do anything by himself to solve the problem or meet the need. God did it! Paul says:

> *Grace be to you and peace from God the Father, and from our Lord Jesus Christ, Who gave Himself for our sins, that He might deliver us from this present evil world, according to the will of God and our Father.*
> (Galatians 1:3,4, King James)

The Cross is not only the centre of the Bible and history; it is the centre of our faith. Unless we have seen the truth and experienced the power of the Cross, then we have not yet come to know the saving grace of Jesus in our lives. To know the meaning of the Cross is to experience the liberating effect of God's power in our own life. It is to grasp the tremendous mystery that to save us; God died for us!

For many people, the Cross has become a decoration or a piece of jewellery. In fact, going by the evidence around, I would say it seems to be a highly popular emblem to wear; either as earrings or as a pendant around the neck. Church buildings are decorated with crosses and altars are bedecked with them. But does all this mean that the real power and message of the Cross is understood and received by as many people? I don't think so! In fact, the true message of the Cross is still an enigma and offence to the majority of people, as it always seems to have been.

> *For the message of the cross is foolishness to those who are perishing, but to us who are being saved it is the power of God.* (1 Corinthians 1:18, NKJV)

A new vision

I recall very vividly one morning when I saw into the real meaning of Calvary in a new way. I was out in the Netherlands leading a conference for members of the Royal Air Force stationed in mainland Europe. We were staying in a Roman Catholic Convent; a superb place with every facility for the meetings. I had a large room with beautiful wood-panelled walls. The decor was such as fitted the sort of building it was and on one wall was a exquisitely carved crucifix. The sight of it provoked me to very mixed feelings and for the next day or so I found myself growing increasingly uneasy about this crucifix—but I couldn't tell why. Until one morning early, when I woke up, it suddenly dawned on me. The figure on the crucifix was too nice!

It was a terrific carving, but the figure on the cross looked like a slightly woe-begotten model of fine manhood. There was none of the horror, none of the violence, none of the

6

shame or profound degradation that went along with Roman crucifixion, but in particular with the crucifixion of Jesus. Things happened to Jesus that went beyond the bounds of regular Roman execution. I couldn't see any real evidence that these things had gripped this artist's heart for all the piety and devotion of the carving. What I saw was a kind of saintly pity. And with that millions have identified.

Behold the Lamb

As I lay in bed looking at the crucifix, I remembered the words of John Baptist when he saw Jesus coming towards him on the banks of Jordan:

> *Behold! The Lamb of God who takes away the sin of the world.* (John 1:29, NKJV)

He had a vision that was different from this adoration. His vision was of murder, of sacrifice. An image taken from the Old Testament which expressed the reality of one standing in another's place. And that is the heart of Calvary!

> Upon that Cross of Jesus,
> Mine eyes at times can see
> The very dying form of One
> Who suffered there for me;
> And from my smitten heart with tears,
> Two wonders I confess—
> The wonder of His glorious love,
> And my own worthlessness.

The vision gripped my own heart and I reached out for my Bible to read again the record of John in his Gospel about the sufferings of Jesus. I also read the words of Isaiah 53 (NKJV):

Who has believed our report?
And to whom has the arm of the Lord been revealed?
For He shall grow up before Him as a tender plant,
And as a root out of dry ground.
He has no form or comeliness;
And when we see Him,
There is no beauty that we should desire Him.
He is despised and rejected by men,
A Man of Sorrows
and acquainted with grief...
...Surely He has borne our griefs
And carried our sorrows;
yet we esteemed Him stricken,
Smitten by God, and afflicted.
But He was wounded for our transgressions,
He was bruised for our iniquities;
The chastisement for our peace was upon Him,
And by His stripes we are healed.

I lay and wept as I saw the mystery again. God dying for me! And I saw something else. I saw that every act and action involved in the death of Jesus had a deep meaning. God didn't let these things happen for nothing. The beatings, the mocking, the spitting, the plucking out of his beard, the crown of thorns gouging his brow, the nakedness and shame, the rejection by the leaders, and then the crowd and the physical exhaustion. All this followed by the horror of Roman crucifixion and then the spear—and out came blood and water. His heart was already burst.

Today we domesticate Jesus and we decorate His cross. But it was nothing like that. We want to hide the horror because it offends us to think that God needed to die for us like that! Am I as bad as that? Is that what people like me do to the most innocent human being ever to have lived? Is this the result of what lies deep in the human heart? The envy, jealousy, malice and pride? And anyway, can't we save ourselves? The Cross says we can't.

Another thought

Then something else came to my mind. If God did all this for me, how much must He love me? This is what the Bible says:

In this is love, not that we loved God, but that He loved us and sent His Son to be the propitiation for our sins.
(1 John 4:10, NKJV)

It's at this point I would disagree with the last line of that great old hymn from which I quoted previously.

Two wonders I confess—
The wonder of His glorious love,
And my own worthlessness.

If it is true that God loved me so much as to allow Jesus to die like this for me, I can't be so worthless in His sight! I may seem useless, I may be helpless, but praise God He counts me precious—worth saving.

You are a chosen generation, a royal priesthood, a holy nation, His own special people, that you may proclaim the praises of Him who called you out of darkness into His marvellous light. (1 Peter 2:9, NKJV)

The Lamb of God

God had already prepared the stage of history for this amazing act of sacrifice. Throughout the experiences of His old people, the Jews and their forefathers, He had expressed in a prophetic manner the work of Jesus. We have already read words from the prophet Isaiah, written over six hundred years before the time of Jesus. And yet who can seriously suggest they are fulfilled to any meaningful degree in any other person but Christ?

The same is true of one of the most powerful types of the Old Testament. Time and again we come across the image of the Lamb. John the Baptist saw it and the Jews of his day knew it. Such language was familiar to them, from their present and their past. Every day in the Temple, lambs were slaughtered in sacrificial rituals; and on one great day of the year, the Feast of Passover, the lamb was slain to remind the people of their great escape from Egypt by the grace of God. The image of the Lamb figures frequently in the Old Testament. Even before the lamb of sacrifice became central to Israelite worship, the lamb is central to the revelation of the Bible.

(a) The Lamb of substitution

Genesis 22 tells the heart-rending account of Abraham being told by God to take his only son Isaac and sacrifice on Mount Moriah. Abraham, man of faith that he was, obeys God and prepares for the journey; and then after three days comes to the spot which God had told him of. Leaving the servants behind, he and Isaac go up the mountain to prepare the sacrifice. Then it dawns on Isaac that they have the wood and the fire, but no lamb. The immortal words of Abraham ring through the centuries with promise:

My son, God will provide for Himself the lamb for a burnt offering. (Genesis 22:8)

The words are deeper than they seem at first reading. It wasn't only that God would provide a lamb. It means what it says, that God will provide *for Himself* a lamb. That is, the choice of the lamb belongs to God, as well as the need for the lamb.

Of course, many, even within the organised Church, object to this idea of substitution. But the Bible is full of it. So full of it that you can't really miss it. The fact is that in Jesus, God provided *for Himself* a Lamb. The choosing was His, not ours. This is the mystery and the greatness of it.

Modern bishops blush at the truth and theologians scorn it. But true men of God have always known it:

> Was it for crimes that I had done
> He groaned upon the tree?
> Amazing pity! Grace unknown!
> And love beyond degree!
>
> Well might the sun in darkness hide,
> And shut his glories in.
> When Christ, the Mighty Maker, died
> For man, the creature's sin.

Isaac Watts

(b) The Lamb of sacrifice

An equally remarkable event in the history of Israel is marked by the Feast of Passover. Here too a lamb features at the centre of the action. On the night of their release from Egypt, the ancient Israelites were instructed by God to prepare a lamb. This became known as the Passover Lamb, because its blood was sprinkled on the doorposts and lintel of each Israelite home as a sign of covenant. When the Lord saw the blood, He passed by that home and the angel of death did not strike the family (Exodus 12:23).

The death of Jesus took place at this very time of year to remind us, vividly, that it is only through the life-blood of Jesus, that we too can escape the consequences of death. Paul in writing to the church at Corinth describes Jesus as *'Christ our Passover'* who has been sacrificed for us (1 Corinthians 5:7).

Such a vivid picture reminds us of what really counts for God in the sacrifice of Jesus. The life is in the blood. Through man's disobedience, sin entered into the world, and; says the Bible, death through sin (Romans 5:12). The first act of a sinful man was a fatal one. Cain slew his brother Abel and shed his blood. That which God had given for life now became the symbol of death. From then till now, death has ruled with an iron hand over the human race and has given room to the power of the devil, who through the reality and fear of death, breeds fear and darkness in the hearts of men. But now all the other sacrifices have been fulfilled. Jesus has died and brings us life.

> *He has appeared to put away sin by the sacrifice of Himself. And as it is appointed for men to die once, but after this the judgment, so Christ was offered once to bear the sins of many. To those who eagerly wait for Him He will appear a second time, apart from sin, for salvation.*　　　　　(Hebrews 9:26–28, NKJV)

(c) The Lamb of suffering
There is no more graphic picture of innocent human suffering than in the prophetic words of Isaiah chapter 53. It is all summed up again in the picture of a lamb:

> *He was led as a lamb to the slaughter,*
> *And as a sheep before its shearers is silent,*
> *So he opened not His mouth.*　　　(Isaiah 53:7, NKJV)

In other places, the Old Testament is equally clear in its portrayal of the sufferings of the Messiah. Take the words of Psalm 22 which so poetically and yet realistically speak of the sufferings which Jesus endured at His crucifixion:

> *Many bulls have surrounded Me;*
> *Strong bulls of Bashan have encircled Me.*

They gape at me with their mouths,
As a raging and roaring lion.
I am poured out like water,
And all My bones are out of joint;
My heart is like wax;
It has melted within me.
My strength is dried up like a potsherd,
And My tongue clings to my jaws;
You have brought me to the dust of death.
For dogs have surrounded me;
The assembly of the wicked has enclosed me.
They pierced my hands and my feet;
I can count all my bones.
They look and stare at me.
They divide my garments among them,
And for my clothing they cast lots.

(Psalm 22:12–12, NKJV)

No one reading words like these with any sense of objectivity, written as they were, so long before the time of Jesus can fail to be impressed by their close reference to what actually took place at the Crucifixion.

The fact is that the sufferings are significant, not just as part of the whole work of salvation, but in their own right. The power of the Cross for us lies in the fact that every detail of the experience of Jesus, in His sufferings, has dynamic reference to us at every point of our need. Ever since the fall of man, Satan has kept men and women under his oppression. They have been bound in chains of sin and sickness. Depression and despair have been the hallmark of human experience. Man has become subject to every kind of suffering and affliction as a result of his disobedience to God and subsequent vulnerability to the devil. On the Cross, every emotional, physical and spiritual suffering of the human race was borne by God in His mercy. The power of these things was carried and broken in the death and resurrection of

Jesus. Through the power of the Holy spirit in us, we may begin to experience the freedom which Jesus won for us through His own sufferings. More of freedom which Jesus won for us through His own sufferings. More of that later!

(d) The Lamb of sovereignty

The image of the Lamb leaps from one end of the Bible to the other. From Genesis right through to the book of Revelation. In the fifth chapter of Revelation we see the Lamb again, not this time suffering or broken, but in triumph. The scene is the end of the ages and the Lamb of God now stands at the heart of God's final purposes in heaven and on earth. He is surrounded with glory and by innumerable crowds of people. Centre stage is a scroll sealed with seven seals. This scroll contains the secret of all that is to happen. But who can open it? Who has the right and the authority? No one, it seems, has the power. Then, an amazing scene takes place. The writer of the vision says:

> *So I wept much, because no one was found worthy to open and read the scroll, or to look at it. But one of the elders said to me, 'Do not weep. Behold, the Lion of the tribe of Judah, the Root of David, has prevailed to open the scroll and to loose its seven seals.' And I looked, and behold, in the midst of the throne...stood* **a Lamb as though it had been slain.**   (Revelation 5:4,5, NKJV)

Can you see the power of this? The Lion of Judah, the Root of David, these are Messianic titles of power and majesty. John turns to see the Lion and *'behold...a Lamb'*.

This is telling us something very important about the Crucifixion of Jesus. Maybe the image of a lamb seems somewhat weak and defenceless. But this is not the purpose of the Biblical picture at all. Yes, it is one of suffering, one of sacrifice, but above all, it is one of triumph.

14

The head that once was crowned with thorns,
Is crown'd with glory now.
A royal diadem adorns
The mighty victor's brow.

T. Kelly

2

'Tis Mystery All

Throughout the centuries, there have been many arguments about the death of Christ. However, there is no disagreement about its centrality. Without the death of Jesus, Christianity is only another religion with a founder who claims to be a divine/human being with miraculous powers. We cannot escape the death of Christ—it stands central to the whole Christian proclamation. The arguments have been about how it can be that God saves fallen man through the death of Jesus. In what way is His sacrifice effective or sufficient?

Many theories have been developed over the years to try to explain how God did this amazing thing. Some have been developed which attempts to appease the human intellect, so that the Cross is understandable to reason. But this can never be. Paul was right when he declared:

> *We preach Christ crucified: a stumbling block to Jews and foolishness to Gentiles, but to those whom God has called, both Jews and Greeks, Christ the power of God and the wisdom of God. For the foolishness of God is wiser than man's wisdom, and the weakness of God is stronger than man's strength.* (1 Corinthians 1:23–25)

The fiercest debate has raged around the question of atonement: how did God satisfy the demands of His own holy nature at the same time as manifesting the depths of His love towards mankind? Any thought that God made Jesus bear the punishment of our sins and take our guilt on Himself as our substitute seems to have caused offence to many thinkers over the years. And so, time and again, they have propounded theories about the death of Jesus which seek to avoid this terrible conclusion. But the conclusion is unavoidable! In the end, there is no escaping the fact that the New Testament writers clearly proclaim that Christ was offered as the sacrifice for our sins:

> *He himself bore our sins in his body on the tree, so that we might die to sins and live for righteousness; by his wounds you have been healed.* (1 Peter 2:24)

Paul highlights the depths of this even further when, in writing to the Galatians, he appeals to the language of the book of Deuteronomy. For him, it is not only a matter of Jesus *taking* our sins upon Himself, rather it is a matter of Jesus *becoming* something for us! This is the depth of Calvary. It is not only something done to Jesus, it is something done *in* Him! Paul says:

> *Christ redeemed us from the curse of the law by becoming a curse for us, for it is written: 'Cursed is everyone who is hanged on a tree.'* (Galatians 3:13)

Sin for us

No Scripture highlights this fact more clearly than 2 Corinthians 5:21:

> *God made him who had no sin to be sin for us, so that in him we might become the righteousness of God.*

A footnote in the New International Version suggests the

alternative: 'sin-offering'—that is, that God made Christ a sin-offering for us. This would echo the type of sin-offering in the Old Testament. But we need to recognise that the type is only a shadow of what is to come and that this image falls short of what *actually* happened in the experience of Jesus. Every major commentator on the text agrees that the import of the words, *'to be sin for us'* is much deeper than the thought implied by the type of sin offering. He *is* our sin offering, as the writer to the Hebrews makes clear:

> *Unlike the other high priests, he does not need to offer sacrifices day after day, first for his own sins, and then for the sins of the people. He sacrificed for their sins once for all when he offered himself.* (Hebrews 7:27)

But He did something that no sin offering ever did. He became our substitute, not only by taking sin *upon* Himself, but by taking our sin *into* Himself. The victory over sin, death and the power of Satan was not only worked *by* Him—it was achieved *in* Him!

This profound Scripture contains all the mystery and wonder of Calvary. How will we ever be able to comprehend what God did for us in the death of His Son? Certainly we should not err on the side of underestimating it! There are certain fundamental issues raised in the light of this Scripture which will help us to see something of the power and wonder of it all.

(a) The difference between sin and sinful

It is of fundamental importance that we understand what Paul is meaning. For too long we have lived with watered-down ideas of what it meant for Jesus to suffer.

Nowhere in the New Testament are we taught that Jesus Himself became a *sinner*. This is what I mean when I stress the difference between 'sin' and 'sinful'. Jesus, in Himself, was not sinful. This is why we speak of Him bearing the penalty of our sin rather than the punishment for sin. He was not punished for any sin of His own—He bore in Himself the penalty for our sins. The writer to the Hebrews makes it clear on more than one occasion that Jesus offered Himself up as a perfect sacrifice without spot or blemish:

> *How much more, then, will the blood of Christ, who through the eternal Spirit offered himself unblemished to God, cleanse our consciences from acts that lead to death.* (Hebrews 9:14)

Philip Bliss captured the thought of that when he wrote the beautiful meditation on the Cross, *Man of Sorrows*. In one verse, he draws the contrast between what we are in our sin and what Christ is in His offering:

> Guilty, vile and helpless we,
> Spotless Lamb of God was He.
> 'Full Atonement!'—can it be?
> Hallelujah! What a Saviour!

God did not deal with the question of sin merely by observing the physical death of His Son. No, Jesus entered into that death! Physical death is the outcome of man's sin and disobedience, but it is not its only effect. Divine judgement and dereliction are the result of sin. Death toward God is the ultimate outcome of sin. Satan's oppression and bondage are the result of sin. Sickness and disease are the result of sin. For man to be delivered from the fact and effect of his sin, the Son needed to take *all this sin* into Himself. This is the most humiliating truth of this necessity. No wonder we are reluctant to carry these thoughts through to their conclusion. What a horrific claim to make with regard to the Son of God! He became sin! We need to come in awe to Calvary, to take our shoes from off our feet, for the place on which we stand is holy ground!

(b) The difference between human and mortal

Part of the problem is that we don't stop to consider the real meaning of the words we use. These two words are terms which we often confuse with each other. To be human, as far as we are concerned, is to be mortal. But is that the truth as far as God is concerned? When God created man, did He create man to be mortal—that is, subject to death? The answer is clearly, no.

Both the book of Genesis and the Epistle to the Romans are explicit as to the source of death. Genesis 3:22 makes it clear that God expelled man from the garden to prevent him from eating the tree of life by which he could live for ever. From this point on, man became subject to death as a judgement from God. Paul is very explicit on the subject when he writes to the Romans:

> *Sin entered the world through one man, and death through sin, and in this way death came to all men, because all sinned.* (Romans 5:12)

But the point is that Jesus Himself was not subject to man's death until He took man's sin into Himself, because death is the outcome of sin. Jesus Himself was not sinful, therefore, He did not live His life under the threat of death as a necessary outcome of sin. Jesus Himself made His position clear in this regard. He was the only man who ever lived who had the authority of life in Him:

> *The reason my Father loves me is that I lay down my life—only to take it up again. No one takes it from me, but I lay it down of my own accord. I have authority to lay it down and authority to take it up again. This command I received from my Father.* (John 10:17,18)

This is the tremendous fact of Calvary: the only One who

had no need to die either spiritually or physically was the very One who took death upon Himself to break its power:

> *Since the children have flesh and blood, he too shared in their humanity so that by his death he might destroy him who holds the power of death—that is, the devil—and free those who all their lives were held in slavery by their fear of death.* (Hebrews 2:14,15)

Charles Wesley writes with tremendous spiritual insight when he proclaims the depths of this:

> 'Tis mystery all! The Immortal dies:
> Who can explore His strange design?
> In vain the first-born seraph tries
> To sound the depths of love divine.
> 'Tis mercy all! let earth adore;
> Let angel minds inquire no more.

That is the truth! On the cross it was the *immortal* who was put to death! Jesus was human but immortal. He took death upon Himself. It was not until He took human sin upon Himself that He entered into the fact of death. This was the struggle of the Garden of Gethsemane. There Jesus wrestled with the awful reality of what was before Him. No man in normal human strength could ever have faced what Jesus faced. Luke tells with great pathos what happened in the Garden:

> *He withdrew about a stone's throw beyond them, knelt down and prayed, 'Father, if you are willing, take this cup from me; yet not my will, but yours be done.' An angel from heaven appeared to him and strengthened him. And being in anguish, he prayed more earnestly, and his sweat was like drops of blood falling to the ground.* (Luke 22:41–44)

It was here in the Garden that Jesus submitted Himself completely to the will of His Father and took into Himself all the reality of man's sin. From that moment forward, He was subject to death.

(c) Born of God, not of Adam

Of equal importance is the debate that has gone on for years about whether Jesus was born of a virgin or not. Some write it off as an irrelevancy. For them, it seems to make no difference to the Gospel. But the Gospel writers themselves are clear about it. Matthew and Luke go to pains to give a detailed account of the birth of Jesus. John records the birth of Jesus in his own way and, in particular, when he speaks of what God does in the lives of those who come to know Jesus through faith, he is describing the truth about Jesus's own birth:

> born not of natural descent, nor of human decision or a husband's will, but born of God. (John 1:13)

The truth of the virgin birth is vital to our understanding of both the life and death of Jesus. It is clear from Scripture that the life Jesus lived was lived in a real body of flesh. There can be no doubt that He experienced real temptations. This was no play-acting. The grounds of His humanity were the same as the grounds of our humanity as far as this is concerned. The writer to the Hebrews makes this clear:

> For we do not have a high priest who is unable to sympathise with our weaknesses, but we have one who has been tempted in every way, just as we are—yet was without sin. (Hebrews 4:15)

The very last phrase makes it clear, however, that there was something about Jesus which *differentiates* Him from all other men. He was not subject to sin and had the power to overcome every temptation which came to His door. Luke chapter 4 is a magnificent exposition of this fact.

But Jesus was not born of Adam! He was born of the Holy Spirit! This is not the case of men as they are born into the world. They take their lineage from the old Adam, they take their weakness from the old Adam, they take their sin from the old Adam! Jesus is the Second Adam, the Man from heaven (see 1 Corinthians 15:45–49). He is like them in body, but not in spirit! Men, in general, do not take on the likeness of the Man from heaven, that is Jesus, until they too are born of God through the Holy Spirit.

Jesus was born of the Spirit and lived in the power of the Spirit. He never knew what it was to sin. In fact, Jesus lived at the level of true humanity; the humanity which God created for Adam and in which he lived until he fell through disobedience. Jesus' humanity was like ours inasmuch as the body Jesus had, was a real body of flesh. It was like ours inasmuch as it was susceptible to temptation, as was the flesh of Adam before he fell. But it was unlike our humanity in that it was governed by the Spirit of God and never knew the reality of sin until the end. This is where we see the immensity of His offering on the cross. At this point, He did something which He had never experienced before; He opened Himself to the reality and effects of sin within His own body. Not His sin, but the sins of all other men, and into Himself He gathered all its awful effects and judgement:

> *God made him who had no sin to be sin for us, so that in him we might become the righteousness of God.*
> (2 Corinthians 5:21)

3

The Power Of The Cross

O loving wisdom of our God!
When all was sin and shame,
A second Adam to the fight,
And to the rescue came.
John Henry Newman

The significance of the Cross does not lie in the physical sufferings for their own sake. Any man who was crucified by the Romans passed through the most excruciating and horrific sufferings. Crucifixion was recognised as a most horrendous form of execution which involved excruciating pain and personal humiliation. But Jesus did not undergo the normal routine of crucifixion. The Scriptures make that clear. Certain things happened to Him which were not normally part of the crucifixion process. For example, before He was sent to the Cross, He was subjected to the public humiliation of a mock trial before Pontius Pilate, during which He was abused, beaten and disfigured.

His beard was torn out and a crown of thorns was placed on His head as a gesture of mockery at His claim to be a king. Even before He appeared in public at His trial, He had undergone severe sufferings in physical and mental terms. In the garden of Gethsemane, He had faced the awful truth that 'this cup' was His cup and it could not be drunk by any one else. The pressure within His spirit was so intense that

He bled from His brow. The blood flowed from His forehead down to the ground.

Likewise, when it came to the end, things were different for Him. The soldiers came and broke the legs of the two criminals who were crucified with Him that day, but when they came to Jesus they saw that He was dead already, so they did not break His legs. Instead, they pierced His side, and blood and water gushed out. This means that Jesus had died literally of a broken heart. His heart had burst and the blood had congealed: the blood and plasma had become separated and when He was pierced, they flowed out from His side.

We cannot begin to speak about the spiritual sufferings. These things are hidden from us, because there is no way we could ever comprehend what it meant for God's Son to be forsaken by His Father. The cry that tore from His lips which echoed the words of Psalm 22, *'My God, my God, why have you forsaken me?'* contains depths of suffering that we will never be able to understand. But what we must see is that none of these things were by chance. Not one incident of the crucifixion of Jesus was by chance. Men took Him, but men were not in charge of the proceedings that day! This is the awesome truth of Calvary: the Father was in control! The Father was offering up His Son 'for every soul of man'! We recoil from the fact, because it only serves to underline ever more clearly the extent of our guilt. But this was the testimony of Peter in the first Pentecost declaration:

> *This man was handed over to you by God's set purpose and foreknowledge; and you, with the help of wicked men, put him to death by nailing him to the cross.*
>
> (Acts 2:23)

For years I failed to see the reality of this. I looked upon the sufferings of Jesus in a general sense. I knew that in some mysterious way the Father had laid my guilt upon Him and that through His sufferings, which included the physical pains of Jesus, I was set free. But I failed to recognise the *dynamic* significance of the sufferings of Christ. Isaiah prophesied, not only that the Messiah would suffer, but that he would *take upon himself* the sin and sickness of man:

> *Surely he took up our infirmities*
> *and carried our sorrows,*
> *yet we considered him stricken by God,*
> *smitten by him, and afflicted.*
> *But he was pierced for our transgressions,*
> *he was crushed for our iniquities;*
> *the punishment that brought us peace was upon him,*
> *and by his wounds we are healed.* (Isaiah 53:4,5)

The power of the Cross for us lies in the fact that every detail of the experience of Jesus in His sufferings has dynamic significance for us at every point of our need. Ever since the fall of man, Satan has kept men and women under his oppression. They have been bound in chains of sin and sickness. Depression and despair have been the hallmark of much human experience. Man has become subject to every kind of suffering and affliction as a result of his disobedience to God. On the Cross, every spiritual and emotional bondage and affliction which Satan has brought to man through man's disobedience has been reversed in the power of Calvary.

The six woes of man

In Genesis chapter 3, we are given insight into the effects of sin. After the Fall of man through his disobedience to God, we are introduced to the sad effects of this disobedience. Whereas man had lived as a free agent in fellowship with

27

God and had been given the authority to rule over everything else on earth, he was now in bondage. Satan had the mastery over him and from that moment on the human race has been subject to all the ills and trials that result from sin. In Genesis chapter 3, we find that man has become subject to *six awful woes*, which have been the source of every pain and affliction of body and spirit that the human race has ever experienced.

The *first* of these is *guilt* and *condemnation*. Both the man and the woman, when they were challenged by God, tried to avoid the guilt. They passed it from one to the other. This has been mankind's failure ever since. It has been the factor that has divided man from man and man from God. Not until we accept our guilt can there be any reconciliation. But our guilt before God is of such a nature that we could never atone for it ourselves. Jesus became our guilt-bearer. He bore our sins in His own body on the tree.

This is why the words of Paul in Romans chapter 8 are so significant:

> *Therefore, there is now no condemnation for those who are in Christ Jesus, because through Christ Jesus the law of the Spirit of life set me free from the law of sin and death.* (Romans 8:1,2)

The *second* woe is *oppression* by the devil. Before man fell, he was not subject to the dominion of Satan. Now that he is separated from God, he is at the mercy of Satan. Satan has in fact become, as the New Testament says, the god of this world who rules and dominates the hearts and minds of men. But the Cross brought to an end the unchallenged power of Satan. Paul speaks of the triumph of Jesus on the Cross against the power of Satan when he writes:

God made you alive with Christ. He forgave us all our sins.... And having disarmed the powers and authorities, he made a public spectacle of them, triumphing over them by the cross. (Colossians 2:13,15, NIV)

The *third* woe is *pain* and *suffering*. This is emphasised in relation to women in particular, who will know pain in childbearing. This epitomises all the pain and affliction to which the human race is subject. Nowhere in the Bible do we hear that sickness and illness are the will of God for mankind. They are the result of sin and find their source in the work of Satan as the outcome of man's disobedience. That is not to say that God cannot use pain and suffering for His own gracious ends in our lives; it is clear that He can. But we know that these are not God's best designs for His children, and in the perfect kingdom of Jesus, all such foreign elements will be thrown away. Peter makes this connection most clearly for us in the New Testament:

He himself bore our sins in his body on the tree, so that we might die to sins and live for righteousness; by his wounds you have been healed. (1 Peter 2:24)

The *fourth* woe is *anxiety* and *care*. Man was sentenced to a life of hard labour. Whereas he had lived in a garden of God's bounty, surrounded by everything he needed for life and health, now he was condemned to difficulty and effort. The very ground was cursed as a result of man's sin:

It will produce thorns and thistles for you, and you will eat the plants of the field. By the sweat of your brow you will eat your food. (Genesis 3:18,19)

It was thorns that made a crown for Jesus, and He wore it for us. He took upon Himself all the agony of spirit and the anxiety of heart that belong to man as he tries to make his own way in the world without God. What a contrast now, is the way of Jesus to the curse of thorns! Because He carried it for us, we are free, in the power of faith, to walk the way of the Kingdom:

The *fifth* woe is *death*. Man was cut off from the source of his life because of his sin. Paul describes this graphically when he writes to the Romans:

> *Sin entered the world through one man, and death through sin, and in this way death came to all men.*
> (Romans 5:12)

This is a fact that needs no independent corroboration! Our cemeteries declare the truth of it and we all know it for ourselves. Death is the result of our sin, and the common lot of all men. Of course, the Scriptures take us one step further. If physical death was the end of it, perhaps that would not be too bad. In fact, for many it would be a welcome finale to a fruitful life. For others, it would be a welcome relief from a life of pain and misery. The sober truth is spelled out by the writer to the Hebrews:

> *Just as man is destined to die once, and after that to face judgement, so Christ was sacrificed once to take away the sins of many people.* (Hebrews 9:27,28)

But in the death of Jesus, the judgement of death has been removed. He has borne the judgement for us. We shall see later what this meant for Him. At this moment, we can see what it means for us:

> *Since the children have flesh and blood, he too shared in their humanity so that by his death he might destroy him who holds the power of death—that is, the devil—and free those who all their lives were held in slavery by their fear of death.* (Hebrews 2:14,15)

30

The *sixth* woe is *rejection* and *separation from God*. The man was cast out from the garden. And man has been a spiritual castaway ever since! It is significant that many of the spiritual hurts we have to deal with today are hurts of rejection. Man at heart is a rejected being. His sin, as the Psalmist rightly perceived, has caused a separation between him and God, the very ground of his being.

The most profound cry on the cross was a cry of dereliction: *'My God, my God, why have you forsaken me?'* Jesus became a derelict for you and me! There was nothing else that could have happened, because in taking our sins into Himself, He thereby put Himself outside the boundaries of the Father's presence.

The power of the Cross lies in the fact that Jesus took all these elements into Himself on the Cross and broke their power. He overcame every negative factor that has ever threatened man and He broke the power of Satan, who masterminds all these forces to bring man to destruction.

United with Him

It is not enough to wonder at the mystery of the Cross, however. For it to be effective in our lives, we need to receive it into our own lives. A few years ago, a member of the Fellowship to which we then belonged gave a prophetic word which brought this challenge home to every one of us:

> Yes! Many hold their hands up in adoration of what I have done, that death, glorious death, supreme sacrifice; their mouths show forth praise. But I say to them, 'Come join me. You must enter into that death with me; you died with me. Don't you see that? I know that you try to please me, but of yourselves you cannot, except that you join me in death. Then you will enter into resurrection life. I tell you that no man can crucify

himself, purge his sins. I alone have paid the penalty for sins.' Therefore we can now say, 'I can do all things in Christ Jesus. It is no longer I that live but Christ lives in me.'

Those words made a great impact in my own life. They reveal the true heart of the work of Christ. It was in the power of the Holy Spirit that He offered Himself up for us (Hebrews 9:14). It is as we allow the Holy Spirit to do the same work of overcoming sin, affliction and the power of death in us that we will enter into the true victory of Calvary.

4

The Full Virtue Of The Cross

I was encouraged to read what Colin Urquhart has to say in his book *Receive Your Healing*. He is speaking about receiving into our own lives all that the Father has made available for us through the Cross of Jesus. So many of us view the Cross as a kind of divine history lesson. The New Testament makes it clear, however, that we are meant to *lay claim on the achievements and provisions that come from the Cross* and which are made real in us by the present work of the Holy Spirit. Faith is laying claim to what the Father offers us through the sacrifice of His Son. Colin puts it like this:

> I have learned to say something like this when receiving the bread: 'Lord, I believe that as I eat this bread, I have received all the virtue of Christ's body, I thank you for the physical strength and healing I receive through His stripes. I thank you for the material provision I have for all my needs through His abundant grace.'

This is a very real and tangible act of receiving the goodness of God. At the heart of it is the belief and recognition that God now sends His Spirit to bring to us in an immediate and personal way *the full virtue of Calvary*. It is the application of the Cross into my life and experienced through faith. There are many occasions in my own life when I need to go right back to Calvary to see that every need has been met in death and resurrection of the Lord Jesus. Satan wants us to live in unbelief and despair and to stop believing that the Father can meet our needs. But God has established His promises and principles in the Cross of Calvary. If God failed to sustain His people and meet them at every point of spiritual, physical and material need, He would be denying the work He has accomplished through His Son. We don't need to find our security in our emotions when it comes to trusting God, we can look to the Saviour and what the Father has accomplished in Him. As Peter rightly says:

> *His divine power has given us everything we need for life and godliness through our knowledge of him who called us by his own glory and goodness.* (2 Peter 1:3)

It is the Father's purpose to enrich us in every way through what He has done for us in the Cross of Jesus.

> *For you know the grace of our Lord Jesus Christ, that though he was rich, yet for your sakes he became poor, so that you through his poverty might become rich.*
> (2 Corinthians 8:9)

In a practical sense, we need to take our stand on the finished work of Christ at every point of our daily experience. Let's remind ourselves again of some of these virtues which are released to us through the death and life of Jesus.

A: The virtue of forgiveness

Self-condemnation is a common feature of our human experience. Many Christian believers suffer from condemnation of spirit. The reality of our daily failures in our walk with God and the pressure of our interaction with other people often leads to feelings of unworthiness and inadequacy. Forgiveness is a fact from God's point of view. In Christ, He has covered all our sins and when we come to Him in repentance and confession, He never fails to cleanse us and give us that sense of freedom and freshness which is our right through the death of our Saviour. But the devil never likes to leave it there. He loves to play on our feelings of weakness and tries to lead us back into condemnation and bondage within our hearts. This is where we need to receive our forgiveness. It is the difference between what the old saints used to call legal and vital truth. Something can be true without us ever entering into the reality of the fact. Sadly, it is the case for many that God has accomplished their full salvation in Jesus, but they never realise it in their own lives. They live in fear and condemnation within their hearts, instead of enjoying the full liberty of sons of God.

Satan tries to convince us that, in some way, we need to pay for our sins. But this is a total contradiction of the teaching of Scripture and the work of Calvary. Jesus has met all our debt and we need to receive our forgiveness in Him.

> Payment he will not twice demand,
> First at my blessed Saviour's hand,
> And then again at mine!

Thank God for full forgiveness!

B: The virtue of provision

I come back to Calvary many times when things seem tough. These are days when Satan tries to whisper in my heart that God has forsaken me. There are moments when he comes and tries to convince me that my Father does not care and that it is useless to trust in a God one cannot see. He tries to show me what a foolish and senseless thing it is to put my trust in an invisible God. He tries to get me to look at the plain, hard and materialistic facts of life and overwhelm me with the sheer audacity of trusting a living God in the middle of such a secular and scientific world.

The devil doesn't mind us believing in God, as long as He is a God who does nothing. After all, belief in such a God answers the spiritual cravings of the human heart. That's why those people who reject the God and Father who is revealed in Jesus need to replace Him with a god of their own manufacture. Satan's aim is to break that relationship of trust which the Holy Spirit brings to life when we are born again through His power. It is by the Spirit that we know God as our Father and it is through Him that we come to God our Father in simple trust and faith:

> *For you did not receive a spirit that makes you a slave again to fear, but you received the spirit of sonship. And by him we cry, 'Abba, Father.' The Spirit himself testifies with our spirit that we are God's children.*
>
> (Romans 8:15,16)

But what has the Cross to do with our trust in God for our daily needs? Paul makes this clear later in Romans chapter 8 when he says:

> *He who did not spare his own Son, but gave him up for us all—how will he not also, along with him, graciously give us all things?* (Romans 8:32)

This is not some sort of prosperity gospel which offers us a slick means towards riches. It is simply the confidence that comes from knowing the heart of the Father who has met our greatest need in the self-giving love of His Son. He is, as James says, the giver of every good and perfect gift, the Father of lights in whom there is no variableness.

C: The virtue of victory

In His death, Jesus accomplished victory for us over sin, death, the world and the power of Satan; the great enemies that haunt the footsteps of every human being. Satan continually tries to bring us into defeat and weakness through these means. We need to be clear of our victory in Him so that we can overcome Satan in his attacks upon our lives.

He has won for us victory over sin
He overcame sin when He overcame death. Death is the result of sin working in us.

The two great weapons of Satan—guilt and fear—are rendered useless in the life of the believer who stands on the finished work of the Cross.

Jesus has won for us victory over the world
The world in this sense does not mean the beauty of God's creation or all the good things which the Father has provided for His children to enjoy. John reminds us of what the world is when he writes in his epistle:

> For everything in the world—the cravings of sinful man, the lust of his eyes and the boasting of what he has and does—comes not from the Father but from the world.
>
> (1 John 2:16)

The world is that satanic system of evil which has permeated God's order and the society of mankind, and which leads men and women into darkness and away from God. But because of the finished work of Christ on the Cross in which He overcame the principalities and powers of this world-darkness, we can share His victory in the present power of the Holy Spirit.

Everyone born of God has overcome the world. This is

the victory that has overcome the world, even our faith.
Who is it that overcomes the world? Only he who
believes that Jesus is the Son of God.   (1 John 5:4,5)

He has won for us victory over Satan

As we will see later in more detail, the Cross was, in fact, the
cataclysmic battle between the power of Satan, and the
power of God. Everything that flows to us out of the Cross
does so because Jesus won the victory. That victory was not
achieved in some dark and secret corner, but in a public
arena for all to see. When Jesus cried out 'It is finished!' He
was not crying out in weakness or despair, but proclaiming
publicly the mighty victory of God. Paul makes it clear that
in Jesus, God has overcome all the powers of darkness and
that they no longer pose a threat to those who stand in faith
in Christ Jesus:

> *God made you alive with Christ. He forgave us all our*
> *sins, having cancelled the written code, with its regu-*
> *lations, that was against us and that stood opposed to us;*
> *he took it away, nailing it to the cross. And having*
> *disarmed the powers and authorities, he made a public*
> *spectacle of them, triumphing over them by the cross.*
> (Colossians 2:13–15, NIV)

D: The virtue of healing

Three major facts convince me that healing of the body is an
integral part of the Father's purpose in the work of Calvary.

First—*God has established the principle of healing in the*
death and resurrection of Jesus.
    Take the Apostle John, for example, and his record of the
resurrection of Jesus from the dead; John writes as an evangelist par excellence. Every point that he makes is a point

with a purpose. He is not merely writing a biography or a history. His purpose is not merely to inform us of events which occurred; he writes with the passion of an evangelist. He is out to present us with the power of the truth about Jesus. He does not wish to leave us impressed with the eloquence or charismatic attraction of a great leader or guru. For John, Jesus equals all the power of God. John's purpose in writing is to convert us, to bring us to following Jesus and knowing His power in our lives:

> *These are written that you may believe that Jesus is the Christ, the Son of God, and that by believing you may have life in his name.* (John 20:31)

This is why his witness is so important. For him, the tomb was empty. Jesus had risen from the dead. The point he makes in chapter 20 verse 9 is very important. The disciples who looked into the tomb, Peter and doubtless John himself, at that moment had not come to realise from Scripture that Jesus should rise from the dead. Their minds were not coloured by presupposition. They walked headfirst into a miracle!

After them comes Mary who stands outside the tomb in tears. She bends over and sees two angels seated where the body of Jesus had been. As she speaks with the divine messengers, another figure appears whom she does not recognise. He asks her why she is crying. Mary thinks that she is speaking to the gardener and it is not until she hears the voice of Jesus saying her name that her eyes are opened to Who it is. The point surely is that Mary did not recognise Jesus because she did not expect to see Him looking as He did. She had last seen His body, hanging on the tree bruised and bloodied. His body was broken and His visage marred and he had been laid in a tomb, wrapped in spices and bandages. He was marked and torn and His physical frame had been savaged by whipping, crucifixion and burial.

But here, He was standing in all the strength and wholeness of young manhood. He had died bruised and broken a few days ago, but now He was raised, healed and whole. We may learn a lesson from the fact that the Father did leave marks on Him which He will bear for all eternity! These were the wound-marks which drove Thomas to his knees in adoration as his unbelief melted into faith. But otherwise the Lord rose triumphant and whole!

When I saw it in this way, I knew in my spirit that we were seeing something that was integral with the work of salvation. From that moment on, healing was the manifestation of God's Kingdom. We don't yet see the Kingdom in all its glory, but when Jesus reigns in the fullness of His power, we will see the fruit of that testimony then. Now we know in part, but thank God, when we see it, our hopelessness is turned to expectation and our unbelief is turned to faith.

Second—*The Scriptures clearly witness to the inclusion of physical healing as part of the work of Calvary in some sense.*

Healing, like other provisions, come to us *through* the Atonement, rather than *in* it. What this means is that the Cross of Christ is the *basis* for every other provision the Father can and will give us according to His will, but there are other factors which control whether these will be given in every case. Some of these factors are obvious to us, for example, when we need to exercise more faith or when our lives inhibit the Father from being as generous as He wants to be. Other factors are hidden and remain a mystery to us at this moment. For myself, I don't object at all to this mystery. It doesn't stop me praying in faith or asking the Father for help in every time of need. I fulfil the commission He has given and, when He makes it clear, I act in faith for healing and for many other provisions. When it is less clear, I stand on Scripture and pray in obedience knowing that I can trust the Lord but I cannot manipulate Him.

The secret things belong to the Lord our God, but the things revealed belong to us and to our children for ever, that we may follow all the words of this law.

(Deuteronomy 29:29)

Isaiah foresaw the breadth of salvation when he said:

Surely he took up our infirmities
  and carried our sorrows,
yet we considered him stricken by God,
  smitten by him, and afflicted.
But he was pierced for our transgressions,
  he was crushed for our iniquities;
the punishment that brought us peace was upon him,
  and by his wounds we are healed. (Isaiah 53:4,5)

These very last words are echoed by Peter when he speaks of the sufferings of Christ.

He himself bore our sins in his body on the tree, so that we might die to sins and live for righteousness; by his wounds you have been healed. (1 Peter 2:24)

It is, I feel, very significant that it is Peter who quotes these very words, because earlier in his own life, he had personal experience of this saving power of God within his own family circle. Jesus healed his mother-in-law from a fever. Matthew tells of that event in his Gospel and in the very same context he quotes the word of Isaiah 53:4;

This was to fulfil what was spoken through the prophet Isaiah: 'He took up our infirmities and carried our diseases'. (Matthew 8:17)

There are many Scriptures from the Old and New Testaments which bear witness to the healing character of God.

41

What is clear is that not only is it in the nature of God to heal, but that the Father purposed to include this within the work of the Cross. Jesus died not only to save our souls, but our whole man; spirit, soul and body.

Third—*the direct testimony of healing today in the power of the Holy Spirit.*

I, like millions of other Christians, was brought up in my Christian life to believe that things like these were special to the early church, that later they died out and that today we are left to accept sickness as part of Christian suffering. We lived with a truncated version of Calvary. We saw the power of Calvary as far as the question of sin was concerned, but we had to be content with half a gospel. So often it led to defeat.

Praise God, I have lived to see it another way! The Scriptures make it clear that God's purpose is not only for the salvation of our souls, but for the salvation of the whole man. He has quickened our spirits and made us alive to Himself in Christ through the Holy Spirit. That is the essential heart of what it means to be a Christian believer. This is what distinguishes the Christian gospel as a whole message from the partial offer of the faith healer or spiritual healer. We are not only, and we might say not primarily, offering physical healing. Physical healing is an integral part of the Good News, but it is not the Good News by itself!

But the Father does want us to know the saving effect of the Cross in our whole lives. This is why in the New Testament such emphasis is put on the truth that our bodies are the temples of the Holy Spirit. God's purpose is that we should live now in the goodness and power of eternal life.

Now and not yet

The fact is that the Cross was the decisive encounter in the battle between good and evil. There Satan was finally stripped of his power and his fate was conclusively sealed. Yet, there is still a war going on! So it is that the decisive work has been accomplished for our healing, but we are not yet fully healed. Every miracle of God's grace is a miracle of promise. It is a type or pointer to what will fully pertain when Jesus comes in His Kingdom glory.

The fact that the battle is won and yet not over, does not inhibit us from engaging in spiritual warfare at every level today; rather it stimulates us in it. So it is with the question of healing, for surely that is part of the battle! We should not be inhibited from praying for those who are sick just because we realise that everything is not yet perfect.

Stand firm in faith

Faith is the principle of discipleship in the present age. God calls us to exercise this faith in responsible obedience in every part of our lives. Sometimes healing is not possible because of failure on our side. We are fallible and our understanding of things is not perfect and often we don't experience what we desire, either because we have come to the wrong conclusions about what we should expect, or we don't believe that God can do it.

The fullness of God's love

Nowhere is unconditional love more fully expressed than in the Cross. John emphasises this when he says:

*This is love: not that we loved God, but that he loved us
and sent his Son as an atoning sacrifice for our sins.*

(1 John 4:10)

We need to be encouraged to come as children to our
heavenly Father. He does know what is best for us. We have
to come to the throne of grace with confidence, so that we
may receive mercy and find grace to help us in our time of
need (see Hebrews 4:16).

5

Principalities And Powers

One really outstanding fact is that the New Testament
nowhere sees the Cross of Christ in terms of defeat. In fact,
rather the reverse. Everywhere there is a shout of victory.
There is a pervading sense of having been set free and being
overcomers through the work of Christ. The whole infant
Church cries out with Paul:

> *We are more than conquerors through him who loved
> us.* (Romans 8:37)

It is evident that this did not come about through a super-
ficial or unreal outlook on life, since these early believers
had to face real difficulties and even overt opposition and
persecution as they stood for their faith. No, for them it
grew out of a certain understanding of what had happened at
Calvary. Yes, the Cross was the place where forgiveness of
sins was achieved and where guilt and death had been overcome. But there was something more. There was a sense
that a great victory had been accomplished over the very real
and personal powers of darkness which held men in bondage. Jesus had been triumphant! In His death, He had
overcome the powers of death and through the light of His
resurrection God had expelled the powers of darkness.

In his very first address at Pentecost, Peter proclaimed the
power of this fact:

> *God raised him from the dead, freeing him from the agony of death, because it was impossible for death to keep its hold on him.* (Acts 2:24)

What might have seemed an awful defeat to others on the outside, was to the believers a tremendous victory on the part of God. John goes so far as to say that this was the chief reason for the coming of Jesus:

> *The reason the Son of God appeared was to destroy the devil's work.* (1 John 3:8, NIV)

We shall see that what happened on Calvary was, as far as Jesus Himself was concerned, the culmination of a warfare that had been taking place since the fall of man. There Satan had enticed man away from God. He had deceived man into the idea that he could live apart from the sovereignty of God and that he could operate as though he himself were God. The devil had appeared in the scenario as the power behind man's sinful actions, and God had then promised him:

> *I will put enmity between you and the woman,*
> *and between your offspring and hers;*
> *he will crush your head,*
> *and you will strike his heel.* (Genesis 3:15)

Now, in the Cross, that word had come home to roost. Jesus was there not only 'dying for every soul of man' but, in a real sense, setting the record straight and affirming whose power is really in control of the universe. This is how Jesus Himself saw it. Shortly before He went to the Cross, He said to His followers:

> *Now is the time for judgement on this world; now the prince of this world will be driven out.* (John 12:31)

The Person of Satan

It has been fashionable in some quarters to pour scorn on the idea of a personal devil and the reality of demons. It has seemed to some so out of keeping with a modern scientific view of things. Writing earlier in the 20th century, one famous theologian said:

> It is impossible to use electric light and the wireless, and to avail ourselves of modern medicine and surgical discoveries, and at the same time believe in the New Testament world of demons and spirits.
>
> (R. Bultmann: Kerygma and Myth, pp 4–5)

But even since the days of Bultmann, the world has changed beyond recognition. We have seen the evil of war as never before in human history. We have witnessed the huge technological advances of modern science at the same time as the degeneration of the planet and the crying need of millions in hunger and despair. We have observed the resurgence of interest and involvement in the occult at the same time as the decline of institutional religion. These facts present us with serious and cogent reasons for believing that the New Testament is telling the truth. There seems no other credible reason for the self-consuming hatred of humanity and the personal bondage that millions find themselves in, than the active work of those evil powers that the Bible describes as Satan and his fallen spirits.

Time and again the New Testament writers affirm this purpose in the coming and dying of Jesus:

> *He too shared in their humanity so that by his death he might destroy him who holds the power of death—that is, the devil—and free those who all their lives were held in slavery by their fear of death.* (Hebrews 2:14,15)

47

Satan is the tyrant, the oppressor who holds men and women in his evil clutches. The Cross is seen as the climactic battle against his power. There Jesus is exposed to the full-blown reality of evil power which seeks to extinguish Him. But He overcomes the powers of darkness and seals the ultimate fate of Satan on the Cross.

All this is highlighted even more clearly when we consider *the sort of terminology the New Testament uses to describe Satan.*

1. The Deceiver

Paul describes the deception of Satan when he speaks to the Corinthians:

> *The god of this age has blinded the minds of unbelievers, so that they cannot see the light of the gospel of the glory of Christ, who is the image of God.* (2 Corinthians 4:4)

The book of Revelation likewise describes him as

> *that ancient serpent called the devil, or Satan, who leads the whole world astray.* (Revelation 12:9)

This is the essence of his dire work. He leads men and women away from the truth of God. Now Jesus told us that the effect of God's truth is to bring freedom. It follows, therefore, that if people are being led into intellectual and spiritual error, they are going to be in some kind of bondage. Jesus Himself described Satan as *'a liar and the father of lies'* (John 8:44).

2. The Accuser

The word 'devil' in Greek *diabolos* means 'slanderer', just the same as Satan in Hebrew carries a strong idea of accusation within it. He is so described in Revelation 12:10 as the one who accuses the brothers. His prime interest is to find some means by which he can bring condemnation and a sense of guilt within our hearts. Of course, in every one of our lives, he finds that it is not too difficult to find breeding grounds of condemnation. In extreme cases, this issues in a deluge of self-condemnation and criticism, until some people feel they have committed the unforgivable sin and so have put themselves outside the orbit of God's mercy. We are not dealing with fairy tales here, but with the reality that is found in the lives of millions of people. They live in an inner prison of bondage and condemnation which threatens to destroy them. Herein lies the fatal madness of those theological opinions which seek to discredit belief in the powers of darkness. Everything, then, has to be interpreted within the human orbit of things and consequently dealt with within the same order. The failure of this world-view is all too apparent around us in the lives of the oppressed and bound.

The New Testament goes much deeper than this and recognises the profound effect of demonic attack and accusation, and presents us just as firmly with the possibility of release and freedom in the power of the Cross of Jesus.

> *Therefore, there is now no condemnation for those who are in Christ Jesus, because through Christ Jesus the law of the Spirit of life set me free from the law of sin and death.* (Romans 8:1,2)

3. The Oppressor

The whole presentation of the Gospels, as well as other scriptures, portray the work of Satan as a work of bondage and oppression. In certain cases, this is specified as being the case (see Luke 8:26ff for example), where men and women are overtly held in bondage by evil spirits who possess them.

The ministry of Jesus is seen as a frontal attack on the powers of darkness. Right at the start of His public ministry, Jesus declared this to be the case when He stood up in the synagogue at Nazareth and read the words of Isaiah the prophet:

> *The Spirit of the Lord is on me,*
> *because he has anointed me*
> *to preach good news to the poor.*
> *He has sent me to proclaim freedom for*
> *the prisoners*
> *and recovery of sight for the blind.*   (Luke 4:18)

John Stott in his important book, *The Cross of Christ*, puts it like this:

> He announced that through him God's kingdom had come...and that his mighty works were visible evidence of it. We see his kingdom advancing and Satan retreating before it, as demons are dismissed, sicknesses are healed and disordered nature itself acknowledges its Lord (p 232).

4. The Tempter

This description of Satan as the 'tempter' is so powerful, because of the fact that this is how he presents himself to Jesus at the outset of His public ministry. The Holy Spirit leads Jesus into the wilderness where He is tempted of the devil (see Luke 4). This may seem a surprising account but, of course, it is so important if we are to share in the victory of Jesus that He is the one in whom the tempter's power is broken.

Ever since Eve, the devil has succeeded in tempting every other son of Adam. Paul even betrays his fear that his very Christian disciples will succumb to the temptation of Satan. He writes to the Thessalonians:

> *I was afraid that in some way the tempter might have tempted you and our efforts might have been useless.*
> (1 Thessalonians 3:5)

That's Satan's strategy. To divert and annul the work of God by drawing people away to some lesser goal or by fixing their eyes on some lesser issue. He tried time and again to entice Jesus away from the fulfilment of the Father's will. The strength of Jesus lay in His obedience to the will of His Father, even to the point of death!

5. The Destroyer

Revelation Chapter 9 presents us with the awesome sight of a destroying locust-like army whose purpose is to spread anguish and despair amongst those they attack. They are led by a destroying angel, their king whose name in Hebrew is Abaddon and in Greek, Appollyon.

This was the name that John Bunyan used to such powerful effect in his *Pilgrim's Progress*. It means 'destroyer'. This is how Jesus Himself described the devil. He said that he was a murderer from the beginning (John 8:44). Satan even tried to entice Jesus to destroy Himself by throwing Himself from the pinnacle of the Temple, but when all other efforts had failed, Satan tried to destroy Jesus on the Cross. The Cross demonstrates the destructive hatred of Satan against all that is good and perfect. That is the hallmark of his work in the lives of individuals and in the world at large. How else can we explain the malevolence and greed that seems to pervade the human scene.

An overview like this helps us to understand the personal nature of the battle. In Colossians 2:15, Paul spells out the reality of this struggle:

> *Having disarmed the powers and authorities, he made a public spectacle of them, triumphing over them by the cross.*

The words he uses are very significant. *First*, he says that on the Cross Jesus 'disarmed' the powers of darkness. At face value, this is strong enough. It means that He took away their weapons and left them powerless. *But, in fact, there is a deeper and even more powerful meaning in the word.* It literally means 'to be stripped off or discarded.' Here, the picture changes somewhat. It is not only the idea of taking away weapons. The deeper thought in the word is that as Jesus hung on the Cross, the demon powers came and clung to Him like a garment. But He discarded them just as someone would discard filthy clothes! Here is the meaning of this victory. These evil forces which cling successfully to other men were stripped off and thrown away by Jesus! He left them like a heap of filthy clothes!

The *second* phrase Paul uses is equally significant. He says that He made a public spectacle of these evil powers. This phrase means that He 'uncovered their nakedness'. That is, He demonstrated on the Cross the real nature of the powers of darkness with all their evil purpose in attacking the goodness of God, but ultimately in their impotence against the power of God. Here was the 'strong man' being bound by the stronger.

The *third* thing that Paul says is that Jesus triumphed over the powers of darkness on the Cross. That is an image that surfaces time and again in the New Testament. Paul uses it to the Corinthians when he speaks of the fact that God *'always leads us in triumphal procession in Christ.'* The picture is of a Roman conqueror returning from a victorious campaign and behind him comes his triumphant army.

The words of John Henry Newman in the 19th century sum it all up so well:

> O loving wisdom of our God!
> When all was sin and shame,
> A second Adam to the fight,
> And to the rescue came.
>
> O wisest love! that flesh and blood,
> Which did in Adam fail,
> Should strive afresh against the foe,
> Should strive and should prevail.

Climax of the ages

Of course, the Cross is the climax of a battle that had been running through the ages. Ever since the Garden when Satan first deceived man, until the coming of Jesus, this warfare had been a reality. In the coming of Jesus, it was intensified as Satan realised his hour was drawing near. And since Jesus it goes on, not in the same way, but in the manner of a retreating foe who knows that his doom is sealed but who shows a grim determination to take as many with him as possible.

We live in the aftermath of Calvary. That's why we have so much trouble with the devil! With the coming of Jesus, we see from the scriptures that demonic activity increased in a manifold way. Here, they were confronted by the unadulterated power of God and the result was a great disturbance in the order of things. We live in the wake of Calvary and the disturbance still goes on, and will go on until the time comes in the plan of God for the final overthrow of the powers of darkness. But as long as men have a choice, they will be susceptible to the inroads of evil. This is why it is so vital that we understand and appropriate for ourselves the victory of the Cross.

It's interesting to note the word that John uses in his letter when he says:

> *The reason the Son of God appeared was to destroy the devil's work.* (1 John 3:8)

The word 'destroy' (katargeo) doesn't actually mean 'obliterate', rather it means to make ineffective or weak. John Stott says, noting that the word is used of barren land or fruitless trees:

> They are still there. They have not been destroyed. But they are barren. When this verb is applied to the devil, to our fallen nature and to death, therefore, we know that they have not been completely 'destroyed'. For the devil is still very active.... It is not, then, that they have ceased to exist, but that their power has been broken. They have not been abolished, but they have been overthrown.
>
> (*The Cross of Christ*, pp 240–241)

We are not left guessing about the reality of this victory because the New Testament is equally unequivocal in announcing the power of the Resurrection. Paul tells us that in His resurrection by the power of the Holy Spirit, Jesus was declared to be the Son of God with power (Romans 1:4). The resurrection was not the victory, it was the confirmation. The victory over the powers of death was achieved on the Cross. When Jesus cried out with a loud voice, *'It is finished!'*, He was not saying 'I'm done for'. He was proclaiming the victory. The work was done. He rose from the dead, because on the Cross *'he destroyed him who has the power of death.'*

His victory and ours

How are we to enter into the victory of the Cross? It is clear from the New Testament that this is meant to happen. We are meant to identify in some way with the triumph of Jesus. In the book of Revelation, He is called the Overcomer; and seven times the promises of God are given to *'him who overcomes'*.

In one brief sentence, Paul lets us into the secret as to the source of our victory:

> *Thanks be to God! He gives us the victory through our Lord Jesus Christ.* (1 Corinthians 15:57)

So the victory for us is a gift. We cannot achieve it by ourselves. Indeed, there is no need for us even to try to achieve what Christ has won for us. It is the Holy Spirit who makes the victory of Jesus real within our lives. It is He who comes as the power of God. That same power that was at work in Jesus and which overcame the powers of evil so effectively in Him, is the power that the Spirit releases within our lives so that we can share in the victory of Jesus. Without this present work of the Holy Spirit, the Cross is merely a history lesson. But in the power of the Spirit, we too can share effectively in the power of Jesus over Satan. John tells us:

> *You, dear children, are from God and have overcome them, because the one who is in you is greater than the one who is in the world.* (1 John 4:4)

Just as in our old lives we felt the effect of Satan's power as he applied the principles of death to our lives, so now we can know the power of the Holy Spirit as He applies the principles of life to our lives.

Principles of Death

What are the principles of death? They are the reality of a broken law which leads to condemnation and guilt. That is the 'curse of the law'; one point of failure brings the whole load of default on our heads. Then there is the reality of a weakened human nature which the New Testament so graphically describes as the 'flesh'. Then there is the fact of death which brings a sense of hopelessness, frustration and fear. Satan finds an immense opportunity in all of these and more, and through them exerts his powerful influence within the lives of unsuspecting men and women. Add to all this the personal and real attack of the demonic bringing sickness, oppression and bondage into the bodies, minds and experience of many, and we can see our dire need to participate in the victory of Jesus.

The principles of life

The Holy Spirit, however, brings the principles of life and makes them real within us. As we are open to Him in obedience to God's Word, we are able to experience the freedom and healing that the victory of Jesus brings us. This is what many fail to realise when we speak of the saving power of Jesus Christ. We are not dealing with propositions. It is not a matter of words. *We are in the realm of personal power.* Just as in His Person, Jesus overcame the powers of darkness, so through the personal power of His Spirit in us we share in that divine triumph. God leads us in triumph, not by telling us something, but by doing something in us! Just as He did something for us on the Cross, so now He does something in us, by the Cross! What does He do in us? The answer is, that He applies the principles of His victory, through releasing His love and power, through enabling us to experience forgiveness instead of guilt, through giving us His strength to overcome the power of Satan and through giving us a willing spirit by which we desire to follow His word and obey His will. In these ways, the effects of a broken law, a weakened nature, a crushed spirit and a darkened mind are overcome and we are released into the power of God.

Deposit of the Spirit

More than all this, the Holy Spirit also leaves us with effective weapons against the ongoing attack of Satan.

i. The blood of Jesus
In Revelation chapter 12, Satan is overcome *'by the blood of the Lamb'*. This speaks of the power of our forgiveness. Through the blood of Jesus, we are cleansed and forgiven. Time and again Satan attacks us on this ground. He tries to draw us back into condemnation. But, as we affirm the power of the sacrifice of Jesus, we remind him and ourselves that we are standing on new ground.

> *If anyone is in Christ, he is a new creation, the old has gone, the new has come!* (2 Corinthians 5:17)

ii. The authority of Jesus
Specifically, this is in the name of Jesus. To know the name is to know the Person. To live in the power of His name is to share in His power and authority. He has been given the name *'that is above every name'*. His name means 'deliverer'

and through His Spirit He releases the power of that name into the life of those who believe in Him. Paul stresses this when he says:

> *Whatever you do, whether in word or deed, do it all in the name of the Lord Jesus.* (Colossians 3:17)

iii. The Spirit of Jesus
We are not left in the struggles by ourselves. Paul puts it like this:

> *If the Spirit of him who raised Jesus from the dead is living in you, he who raised Christ from the dead will also give life to your mortal bodies through his Spirit.* (Romans 8:11)

These words don't only apply to a future resurrection, but to a present fact. The fact is that the Spirit of Jesus dwells in us and He gives us the power to overcome in His strength.

iv. The word of Jesus
It was in the power of what God had said that Jesus Himself confronted and overcame the temptation of the evil one. The Holy Spirit brings the word of God alive in our hearts. Jesus counselled His disciples to remain in His word. Paul reminds us of the importance of the power of the word of God in our stand against the wiles of the devil:

> *...take the helmet of salvation and the sword of the Spirit, which is the word of God.* (Ephesians 6:17)

The word of God becomes our confession and confounds the doubts of the enemy. This is the secret of the victory of the 'young men' to whom John speaks in his Epistle:

I write to you, young men,
because you are strong,
and the word of God lives in you,
and you have overcome the evil one.   (1 John 2:14)

6

The Afflictions Of Christ

Is it nothing to you, all ye that pass by?
behold, and see if there be any sorrow like unto my
sorrow. (Lamentations 1:12, King James)

Suffering is a fact of life. To those outside of Christ, it is an enigma; to those who are in Christ, it is a necessity! There can be no whole view of discipleship which does not take suffering into its perspective. We are surrounded by it on every hand and we experience it daily in our walk with God.

A: The facts of life?

Suffering is not the same for the believer as for the unbeliever, however. To the person who has not experienced the love of God in Christ for himself, the fact of all the suffering in the world may be the very thing that prevents him from finding God. Why does a God of love allow all these things to happen? How can there be a God of love with such horror and tragedy going on? Questions such as these are wrung from the hearts of well-meaning people who don't know God's love at first hand for themselves. The person who has seen the reality and meaning of the Cross has a very different attitude to the question, although he may also experience the reality of suffering.

Whilst we need to sympathise totally with men and

61

women in their distress and identify with them in their efforts to alleviate suffering, we must not be tempted to begin the discussion at the same level of humanistic thinking. The Cross reveals certain facts to us which inform us at a deeper level of reality altogether. For example, it reminds us above everything of the *awful fact of man's own responsibility* for much of the mess we find ourselves in. The Bible, time and again, makes a direct link between the world and man's responsibility in it. Man was created as a responsible agent by God and given the government of every created thing. Man's failure to carry out that responsibility is reflected tragically in the distortion and tragedy which we see all around us.

C.S. Lewis once said:

> It is man, not God, who has produced racks, whips, prisons, slavery, guns, bayonets and bombs; it is by human avarice or human stupidity that we have poverty and overwork.

> (*The Problem of Pain*)

We would have little difficulty in working that thesis out for our own day. Although we express shock and horror at the millions who are threatened with death by hunger and disease in the Third World, it is fairly plain that with a different set of values in operation and a change of will and heart on all sides, the problem would be reduced to the point of insignificance.

The Cross, above all, *shows us the magnitude of our sin.* The Scriptures teach us that it was because of sin that Jesus died, but the manner of His death shows us just what sin is like. Jesus has been universally acknowledged as a great and innocent man. At the very least, men have seen in Him a symbol of purity and goodness. And yet men took Him and cruelly extinguished His life in one of the most cruel ways ever devised. that is what sin does—it corrupts and distorts, it destroys and opposes anything intrinsically good. Sin is at the root of all suffering in our world today, because it is a world that no longer manifests the harmony, balance and beauty in which God created it.

At a deeper level still, the Cross *is a battle for control*. The world lies under the control of Satan. He has become the '*god of this world*' ever since man relinquished his stewardship of Creation. Man's sin gave Satan the opportunity he had been waiting for to take over and pervert the goodness of God's own Creation. It was almost like his evil revenge for the judgement that had been passed on him when he was thrown out of heaven. But the Cross was the reversal of that power, and now Christ is King and His Kingdom rules over all!

The Cross declares, of course, that *God is not indifferent to suffering*. It is no accident that at the heart of the Christian proclamation stands the greatest example of innocent suffering the world has ever known. But it is more than an example of innocent suffering—it is God taking suffering into His very heart! The prophet Isaiah caught the pathos of that when he said: '*Surely he took up our infirmities and carried our sorrows*' (Isaiah 53:4).

B: These momentary troubles

The New Testament never makes light of suffering; it accepts it as a fact of life! The Christian walks in the way of the Cross, and this means, not only speaking about it, but experiencing it:

> *It has been granted to you on behalf of Christ not only to believe on him, but also to suffer for him, but also to suffer for him.*   (Philippians 1:29)

The history of the Church started with two great waves: first, the wave of power as the signs and wonders of the Holy Spirit swept through the world; then the wave of persecution which followed in the wake of the first wave. We tend to overlook the fact that the tremendous success of the missionary movement of which the Acts of the Apostles speaks was matched only by the ferocity of the opposition which it encountered.

The Christians went out preaching the Cross, but it was a real part of the declaration that they also *experienced the Cross*. Peter underlines this fact when he writes:

> *To this you were called, because Christ suffered for you, leaving you an example, that you should follow in his steps.* (1 Peter 2:21)

(a) The reality of suffering

No one has ever achieved anything for God without knowing the reality of what the Scriptures call 'the afflictions of Christ' in their lives. The trouble is that we only see the outside of people's lives. We see the fruit of their ministry, we see the effectiveness, we see their success, but we rarely see their suffering. Suffering is rarely seen like that. It is done in secret, in the secret of the home or in the secret of the heart. The greatest and most intense suffering is a highly private affair.

The Church did start in the midst of suffering that was very public. We will experience that as well. Before many days, the apostles were put in prison. Before long, Stephen was stoned to death and the Church in Jerusalem came under intense pressure. It is clear that many persecutions and physical afflictions befell the early Christians as they spread out with the gospel. And that has been the case ever since. No generation has been without its martyrs somewhere in the world. The blood of the saints is the seed of the Church.

Read Paul as well and listen to the anguish of his heart

and we can see something of the deep and private anguish of his soul. At times, he is suffering intensely from the pain of misrepresentation or misunderstanding. At other times, his spirit is ploughed by the disappointment of a Demas or John Mark who has chosen a different path from himself. It is difficult to know what was hardest for Paul to bear—the physical pain of the beatings and scourging, or the spiritual pain and hurt of wounds caused by malicious gossip or jealousy among the brethren.

Suffering for Christ is a fact of life for all those who take their discipleship seriously. The last part of chapter 11 of Hebrews shows us to what extent that fact is sometimes true in the lives of those who are faithful to God:

> *Some faced jeers and flogging, while still others were chained and put in prison. They were stoned; they were sawed in two; they were put to death by the sword. They went about in sheepskins and goatskins, destitute, persecuted and ill-treated—the world was not worthy of them.* (Hebrews 11:36–38)

It will be clear already that suffering is not directly equivalent to sickness or illness. I have no doubt that illness is sometimes part of suffering, but the two are not co-extensive. Sickness may be part of suffering for a Christian, but sickness healed does not mean suffering necessarily removed, because the suffering may involve elements much wider than the sickness.

(b) The occasions of suffering

> *If you suffer as a Christian, do not be ashamed, but praise God that you bear that name.* (1 Peter 4:16)

Chapter 4 of 1 Peter speaks a great deal about this question of suffering as a Christian. It encourages us to rejoice in our trials because through them we are participating in the *suffering of Christ* (v 13), and it exhorts those who suffer *according to God's will* (v 19) to commit themselves to their faithful Creator and continue to do good.

It is clear, therefore, that there is suffering which *is* according to the will of God; it is equally clear that, on occasions, we suffer things that are not God's will. For example, when Paul wrote to the Corinthians, he had to remind them that some were suffering sickness which was not according to the will of God. This was because they were playing fast and loose with the truth of the Lord's table and bringing disgrace on the holy things of God and on themselves. The result of this was that some of them were ill and some had even died as a result of their sickness (see 1 Corinthians 11:27–32).

This leads us to remind ourselves that God will use illness and suffering, if need be, as a means of discipline within our lives. This does not mean that all illness is discipline or due to sin, as we shall see, but it does cause us to acknowledge the right of our heavenly Father to deal with our waywardness in whatever way seems best to Him to achieve His best ends in our lives:

> *My son, do not make light of the Lord's discipline,*
> *and do not lose heart when he rebukes you,*
> *because the Lord disciplines those whom he loves,*
> *and he punishes everyone he accepts as a son.*
>
> (Hebrews 12:5,6)

There are a number of circumstances and reasons which give rise to the fact of suffering in our experience. The school of suffering has many classrooms and it seems as though we may well need to pass through them all before we can say that we have graduated from this all-important school of life.

Suffering sometimes arises from the *cost and rigours of*

serving the Lord. We need to be clear about this. God has promised all that we need to fulfil His will, but there is a cost that needs to be borne to make this service effective. The experience of Paul makes this clear inasmuch as he suffered many hardships and his body often bore the marks of his ministry. It could be argued that Epaphroditus, Timothy and Trophimus, who are all noted as having suffered illness, were bearing in their bodies the marks of Christ. Maybe, of course, they were like some of us—not as careful as they should have been in the stewardship of their bodies, or maybe they suffered from the common Christian worker's syndrome of having over-taxed themselves to the point of physical and spiritual protest. The need for this balance is, itself, part of the pressure which can give rise to trial in a personal and spiritual sense.

Suffering sometimes arises as a result of *overt persecution and opposition*. One cannot read 2 Corinthians chapter 11 without being moved by the sheer tenacity of the apostle Paul as he battled on against overwhelming odds to take the gospel throughout the world in obedience to Christ. He describes in vivid terms the imprisonments, the flogging, beatings, stonings, shipwrecks, dangers, bandits, exhaustion, hunger, thirst and exposure he faced, as well as the inward spiritual pressure from the many churches under his care. Then to crown it all, he has to endure his *'thorn in the flesh'* which he describes as *'a messenger from Satan'*. This thorn has been the subject of more debate than almost any other feature of Paul's experience. It is fashionable today to regard it as a person rather than a physical ailment. I prefer to stay with the traditional understanding that it was some physical ailment or affliction. When we take a firm position that a servant of God such as Paul could never have been chronically afflicted like this in a physical way, we are on dangerous ground. It is more important, surely, to see that Paul knew how to obtain the victory over this, as over every other element of suffering he ever experienced:

Therefore I will boast all the more gladly about my weaknesses, so that Christ's power may rest on me. That is why, for Christ's sake, I delight in weaknesses, in insults, in hardships, in persecutions, in difficulties. For when I am weak, then I am strong.

(2 Corinthians 12:9,10)

Suffering comes *as a test to our faith*. Both James and Peter agree that this is an important feature of our spiritual life:

Now for a little while you may have had to suffer grief in all kinds of trials. These have come so that your faith— of greater worth than gold, which perishes even though refined by fire—may be proved genuine and may result in praise, glory and honour when Jesus Christ is revealed. (1 Peter 1:6,7)

It is my experience that this is true, not only in the general sense of the testing of what I believe, but in the particular tests of faith. Whenever I have been called forward into a step of faith, I have usually found that somewhere in it there has been a measure of testing. It is through the most trying difficulties that we become most conscious of God, and it is when we are delivered from the greatest trials that our faith is most strengthened and upbuilt.

Suffering is used to *perfect us in service*. Hebrews 2:10 is a scripture which has puzzled many people. It speaks of the life and ministry of the Lord Jesus:

In bringing many sons to glory, it was fitting that God, for whom and through whom everything exists, should make the pioneer of their salvation perfect through suffering.

How is it possible, they ask, that the Lord Jesus, who was

always sinless and perfect, could be made any more perfect through suffering? Of course, the answer lies in what you think being made perfect involves. There is no question; Jesus did not need to be made more perfect in a moral sense; He was sinless and good in every way. But He did suffer, not only on the Cross, but throughout His life He suffered the malice and mistrust of men around Him, He suffered the misunderstanding of His own kith and kin. Long before He hung on the tree, inward and personal suffering was no stranger to Him. Through this He became *perfectly equipped* to be the Saviour of men. He entered into their sufferings; He knew their hearts and shared their sorrows. So He was made perfect as the author of salvation.

In the same way, we are made perfect. Unlike Jesus, we will never be morally perfect until we get to glory. But *we are perfected* for our work of ministry and service to others. God uses suffering as a way to bring us to that point of moral and spiritual victory where we can stand in the strength of Christ and away from dependence on the things of the flesh:

> *Therefore, since Christ suffered in his body, arm your-*
> *selves also with the same attitude, because he who has*
> *suffered in his body is done with sin. As a result, he does*
> *not live the rest of his earthly life for evil human desires,*
> *but rather for the will of God.* (1 Peter 4:1,2)

Suffering is a *deep means of ministry to others*. Paul underlines this when he speaks to the Corinthians. It is not the suffering by itself which is effective, but suffering coupled with the comfort and help received from God. When this is felt by other people, they receive the depth and reality which the process of suffering has brought and they also receive the overflow of the comfort which God has given:

> *We can comfort those in any trouble with the comfort we*

ourselves have received from God. For just as the suffer-ings of Christ flow over into our lives, so also through Christ our comfort overflows. (2 Corinthians 1:4,5)

(c) The afflictions of Christ
The full impact of this theme can be felt in some words which Paul uses when he describes his own outlook to the Colossians. He says:

> *I fill up in my flesh what is still lacking in regard to Christ's afflictions, for the sake of his body.*
> (Colossians 1:24)

Is Paul saying that there was something incomplete about the sacrifice of Jesus with regard to the forgiveness of sins? Does it need something still to happen in Paul and perhaps in every other Christian who follows him to atone for sin? I think not. To suggest such a thing would be a direct contra-diction of what Paul himself teaches elsewhere, and indeed, to what he teaches in this very letter—namely, that by the death of Christ, God has made available full forgiveness from sin and freedom from spiritual bondage for all who believe in Him.

What does Paul mean then? *First*—we may recall the incident on the Damascus road through which Paul became a Christian. The ascended Christ, who appeared to him then identifies Himself to Paul (then Saul) as *'Jesus, whom you are persecuting'* (Acts 9:5). Now it is clear that Paul never persecuted Jesus personally, so what these words signify is that when Paul as Saul of Tarsus was persecuting the believers, he was, in fact, in them, persecuting Jesus. So every time Paul himself now experienced persecution, it was as though Jesus was being persecuted in him.

Second—we can remember how Paul described his own ministry in 2 Corinthians chapter 4, where he said that the treasure of the gospel was held in jars of clay (v 7). He goes on in that passage to describe the hindrances and constrictions which he experienced day by day. It is almost as though the love of Christ needs to be incarnated into the lives of His servants, so that others might have a live object lesson of God's love for them:

> *We always carry around in our body the death of Jesus, so that the life of Jesus may also be revealed in our body.*
> (2 Corinthians 4:10)

I remember once hearing a well-known American Christian leader who told of an incident in his own life. On one occasion, a famous preacher was leading some meetings in this man's home town. He had wanted to hear him preach for years, but to his disappointment he found that his diary was full over the period when the preacher would be there. This man asked his son to go in his place to the meeting. Afterwards, the father asked the boy what he thought of the famous preacher. The son thought for a moment, and then told his father all that was good about him. Then he stopped and after a time said, 'There was only one thing wrong: he hasn't suffered enough!'

People need, not only to see the fruit of our ministry, they need to be able to discern the process of perfection. It is this process of suffering and its effect in our lives that is so valuable for others. It keeps us from pride and it enables them to see how deeply God needs to work in a person's life before fruitfulness of any measure is possible:

> *The God of all grace, who called you to his eternal glory in Christ, after you have suffered a little while, will himself restore you and make you strong, firm and steadfast. To him be the power for ever and ever. Amen.*
> (1 Peter 5:10)

7

Take Up Your Cross

I remember many years ago being greatly challenged by the testimony of a young American missionary. He wrote some words in his diary not long before he died. The words are even more significant in the light of how he died. His name was Jim Elliot and he was murdered by members of the Auca tribe in Ecuador while he and some fellow missionaries were attempting to make meaningful contact with the tribe. He wrote:

> He is no fool
> who gives what he cannot keep
> to gain what he cannot lose.

1. The cost of commitment

The words of that young missionary have always lived for me as the epitome of what Jesus meant when he said:

> *If anyone would come after me, he must deny himself and take up his cross and follow me. For whoever wants to save his life will lose it, but whoever loses his life for me and for the gospel will save it.* (Mark 8:34,35, NIV)

This is the challenge of the Cross. It is the challenge to radical living and a new set of values. At the heart of the

Cross is disruption and death in the light of which all other things are brought into perspective. The Cross has become the supreme symbol of self-sacrifice. But it is not sacrifice for its own sake. It is the sign of commitment to the perfect will of God. Many have looked upon the crucifixion of Jesus as a noble sacrifice, without having any conception of what it was really about. And so they have considered it a waste, a pity, a shame. God's sacrifices are never wasted, however. They bear great fruit. The writer of the letter to the Hebrews knew this when he exhorted his readers to follow the way of Jesus:

> *Let us fix our eyes on Jesus, the author and perfector of our faith, who for the joy set before him endured the cross, scorning its shame, and sat down at the right hand of God.* (Hebrews 12:2)

After every crucifixion, there's a resurrection as far as God is concerned.

2. The end of the old

Paul puts it in his own words in his letter to the Galatians when he says:

> *I have been crucified with Christ and I no longer live, but Christ lives in me. The life I live in the body, I live by faith in the Son of God, who loved me and gave himself for me.* (Galatians 2:20)

In a very personal sense, Paul sees himself as being involved in the crucifixion of Jesus. The crucifixion for him was the end of the principles which dominated his old way of life. The very Cross which stands as a bridge between fallen man and a holy God, also stands as a separation between the new person in Christ and his old way of life. A.W. Tozer put it well when he wrote:

> The old cross is a symbol of death. It stands for the abrupt, violent end of a human being. In Roman times, the man who took up his cross and started down the road was not coming back. He was not going out to have his life redirected, he was going out to have it ended.

Through the work of the Holy Spirit in us, we enter into the reality of this death to the old. The release of the resurrection power of God cannot be a reality unless there is this radical cutting off from those powers which dominate and direct our old lives. It is this process of identification with the death of Jesus which Paul says leads to that experience of His new life.

> *If we have been united with him in his death, we will certainly also be united with him in his resurrection. For we know that our old self was crucified with him so that the body of sin might be rendered powerless, that we should no longer be slaves of sin—because anyone who has died has been freed from sin.* (Romans 6:5–7)

The Cross spells the end of our old way of living—following the impulses of our old nature and the dominion of the powers of evil. Through the dislocation which the Holy Spirit effects in us as we open ourselves to Him, we are cut off from the old and opened up to the power of a new life in Jesus.

3. Something or nothing

> *God chose the foolish things of the world to shame the wise; God chose the weak things of the world to shame the strong. He chose the lowly things of this world and the despised things—and the things that are not—to nullify the things that are.* (1 Corinthians 1:27,28)

I am so often aware of how much needs to change if I am to know God's power at work within me to anything like the extent He desires. Satan is always making his appeal to that inbuilt urge that we all have, to be something. Even in terms of our Christian lives, that basic urge is such a strong force that it often motivates our very service for God. From the first day that I became a Christian, I have wanted to be something for God: preacher or evangelist, whatever it might be; that was my whole ambition. Something for God. Looking back, it's easy to see just how much of the flesh was mixed with that desire and how often the devil was able to play on that inward urge. The trouble is that even Spirit-filled Christians find the flesh and the Spirit to be so mixed together, and the balance is so loaded in favour of the flesh, that the work of the Spirit is all but annulled or dissipated. This is the tragedy of our lives. There is so much potential for God, but we give Him so little room to work. As I look back, even to recent times, I become filled with great sadness, because I can see that so much of my Christian life was really the old life lived in religious or spiritual guise. I realise just how far away I am from what God desires me to be. How closed we are to the reality of God and His glory, and how sullied our lives are by the self-interest and pride that dominate our experience! Sometimes this fact hits me so hard that it almost obliterates me at a spiritual level, and I have to struggle in the spirit to regain any equilibrium and feeling that anything is worthwhile.

The trouble is that God really can't use 'somethings'. It is in the lives of those who are described in Scripture as being 'nothing' that God has chosen to manifest His power and glory. The fact is that we need to die to ourselves in a very radical way. Even much of our so-called spirituality and charismatic religion has done little but develop a heightened self-consciousness in which we never rise beyond ourselves or our problems to glimpse the glory of God.

God's visual aid

Angie is the wife of John Hindmarsh, one of my team. I met her one day outside my office. I could see at a glance that something had affected her profoundly. She told me what had happened and I knew straight away exactly what it was all about.

Angie had newly come in from driving her car. As she was coming here, she had witnessed something that deeply upset her. A lorry had just run over a collie dog. It was a terrible mess and at first glance she imagined that the dog involved was their own pet collie, Jess. It gave her a start, but as she observed the scene, an amazing thing happened to her. It was as though the Holy Spirit took over and used the incident as a visual aid for Angie, and she almost heard the voice of the Lord saying in her ear, 'That's you down there. You're dead.'

It was this that was having such a drastic effect on her when I met her. By then she knew it was not her own dog that had been killed, but that wasn't important to her. She had gone through a transformation in that moment. It was like a personal crucifixion, and it has led her to a whole new sense of God and a willingness for the release of God's power in her life. The old Angie had been very concerned with her place in life and with the status of her husband's ministry, but now she came to see that to have any true ministry, we all need to die to such attitudes and be open to

God. The important thing that she now realised was that it was not her points of weakness that had to be dealt with by God, but those very areas that she had considered her points of strength.

She entered into that depth of understanding that some of us around her had been experiencing during the months before; the reality of a death deep within the spirit. Not a death of the spirit, but a deep inner awareness that if we wanted to see and know the power of God, then much that we had previously counted as valuable in our lives would need to go. God had used this grotesque incident to bring home to Angie's spirit the need for such a death within herself.

That illustrates a basic truth. We all need to come through to that point of brokenness and death until we feel there is nothing left. Only then can we begin to be open to the new thing that God wants to do within and through us.

This is exactly my own experience. It is not our weaknesses that God needs to deal with, but those facets of our personalities and experience that we often regard as our strong points. They are often the places where we don't feel the need for heavy dependence on God and in which we feel strong and self-confident.

The ways of God are deep and mysterious, and they start with the demolition and death of everything in our lives and ambitions that come from the flesh. There is no doubt that the New Testament is right when it identifies the flesh as our greatest enemy and God's biggest problem. It has continually to be dealt with and overcome. Even though we are to *reckon* it dead (Rom 6:11), there is no doubt that in real terms it is still active; and if we want to know God's power within our lives, something radical needs to change with our fleshly selves.

Ointment poured forth

I have come to see in a completely new light the words of Paul which head this section. God has chosen the things that are nothing. Not only those who *have* nothing, but those who *are* nothing. It is not a matter of social status or degree; it is much deeper than that. If we are really keen to know the ways of God's power in our lives, then we need to walk the way of Jesus. It is the way of death. We need to be broken. Only after that can God put healing *into* our lives so that He can pour His healing *out* through our lives. So often what pours out is not the healing balm of God, but the sheer blatant arrogance of the flesh—the old nature wrapped up in religious guise. The pride of life is dressed up to make it look godly or the ambitions of the old self are revamped to make them sound holy.

God wants to put His fragrance into our lives but, as when Mary anointed the feet of Jesus, so the jar has to be broken before the ointment of the Holy Spirit can flow out from us.

God's way seems so utterly absurd. But when you examine it you know that it is the only way. Unless you become nothing, God will never make you anything.

The mark of God

I often reflect on the experience of Jacob at the brook Jabbok (Gen 32:22–32). That is where he met with God in such a special way. Alone that night he wrestled with the Messenger of God right through until the day broke. Jacob refused to let God go until He blessed him. To stay in that struggle cost Jacob everything he was and had. It cost him his old name and it cost him his strength. No longer was he called Jacob, but Israel, because he was the one who had power with God. God smote him in the tendon of his thigh and from that day he bore the mark of this meeting with God in his body. There was a lameness about the new Jacob, but his lameness was his strength. No wonder he called the name of the place Peniel, 'face of God', for he had met God face to face and yet lived to tell the tale.

No incident more portrays how we need to meet with God, to be touched by the power of God and burned by the holiness of God. To know that God has looked into our lives and in His love has spared us—that is true brokenness. Brokenness like that is not weakness. It is the very source of strength in the spirit. After such a meeting, things never look the same again. I would say in fact that his is the source of the greatest power in the whole world. There is nothing stronger than a man who has been touched by God. He has nothing left to prove and nothing more to fear. The old fight has gone, the old fire has been put out and the old aggression has been laid to rest. Inside there is an emptiness that only God can fill. It is not the emptiness of nothingness or meaninglessness, it is the emptiness of God. Outwardly there is a weakness that only God can make strong. I believe this is the way forward. For too long we have engaged in the enterprise of the kingdom of God in ways that look suspiciously like a copy of the old order of things.

The old values don't seem to matter any longer. One thing, of course, that we need to guard against is the other extreme into which we can be led by Satan—to believe that nothing at all matters any more, as though everything in life has been completely devalued by this kind of experience. Not at all. What we need to realise is that the Holy Spirit comes as God's great assayer. He is here to show us God's true values and to lead us into a new and deeper appreciation of all the good things that find their source in the creative hand of the Father—not only 'spiritual' or 'religious' things, but every good and perfect gift with which He surrounds us. This brings a completely new sense of appreciation and thankfulness into life and enables us to enjoy the things that God has freely given us.

In such brokenness, there is a deep sense of dislocation. Paul experienced the very same thing. He wrote:

*I have been crucified with Christ and **I no longer live**, but Christ lives in me. The life I live in the body, I live by faith in the Son of God, who loved me and gave himself for me.* (Galatians 2:20)

8

On The Third Day

How tremendous is the power available to us who believe in God. That power is the same divine energy which was demonstrated in Christ when he raised him from the dead and gave him the place of supreme honour in Heaven. (Ephesians 1:19 [J.B. Phillips])

The essence of the Cross is made good in us through the power of the Resurrection. Time and again, the New Testament affirms this link. Paul says:

If Christ has not been raised, your faith is futile; you are still in your sins. (1 Corinthians 15:17)

In his first address on the day of Pentecost, Peter preached the Resurrection as an integral part of the work of salvation:

But God raised him from the dead, freeing him from the agony of death, because it was impossible for death to keep its hold on him. (Acts 2:24)

a. A historical fact

Although many have tried to pour cold water on the fact of the Resurrection of Jesus and others have attempted to play down the physical reality of the Resurrection by substituting some kind of 'spiritual' resurrection in its place, the New Testament is unequivocal in its witness and would require significant alteration to make it say different.

Jesus Himself spoke of the resurrection of His body when He contended with His Jewish opponents:

> *Destroy this temple, and I will raise it again in three days.* (John 2:19)

John is at pains to make clear that Jesus was not speaking about the Temple building, but about the temple of His body. Jesus laid claim to the absolute authority with regard to His life:

> *The reason my Father loves me is that I lay down my life—only to take it up again. No one takes it from me, but I lay it down of my own accord. I have authority to lay it down and authority to take it up again. This command I received from my Father.* (John 10:17,18)

Many different theories have been propounded by the opponents of Biblical truth to explain away the physical Resurrection of Jesus. Some suggest that He swooned on the Cross and by some miracle of superhuman strength recovered in the tomb to free Himself and come out. Others have suggested that someone stole the body—either the disciples or someone else. If it was someone else, one wonders why they did not make the fact known a few days later when the disciples were making what would have been the very rash claim that their Jesus had risen. If the disciples, one wonders why so many were willing to give their own lives in martyrdom for the sake of a hoax?

On a different tack, some have suggested that the disciples were experiencing hallucinations as a result of the shocking events surrounding the Crucifixion. This, it is propounded, left them in a daze with the bottom knocked out of their world, and some sort of false hope or wistful thinking led them to have 'resurrection' experiences which had no basis other than their own imagination.

Still others say the Jews or the Romans, the two main parties involved in getting rid of Jesus, were behind it. They removed the body either to prevent rioting or to try and prevent the birth of a new messianic movement which would destabilize the situation. In either case, the Jews and the Romans were exceedingly silent on the day when Peter made his claims that Jesus had risen from the dead. He said it right there in Jerusalem, the centre of the action, where thousands must still have had a fresh memory of the events of the Cross. Not one voice, however, was raised against the facts. All that was needed was a body, almost any body of a young man who had been crucified, because after undergoing what Jesus did, the body would have been marred almost beyond recognition. There was no body, however, because the facts were as they had been claimed—Jesus was risen from the dead!

The Scriptures are at pains to point out the physical as well as the spiritual side of the Resurrection. Instances like His encounter with Thomas when Jesus invited the doubting disciples to reach out his hand and see the evidence. Or the time when Jesus came to a group of His disciples who were startled and frightened because they thought they had seen a ghost:

> *Look at my hands and my feet. It is I myself! Touch me and see; a ghost does not have flesh and bones, as you see I have.* (Luke 24:39)

Writing many years later, Paul recalls the power of the testimony to the Resurrection.

> *For what I received I passed on to you as of first import-*
> *ance: that Christ died for our sins according to the*
> *Scriptures, that he was buried, that he was raised on the*
> *third day according to the Scriptures, and that he*
> *appeared to Peter, and then to the Twelve. After that, he*
> *appeared to more than five hundred of the brothers at the*
> *same time, most of whom are still living, though some*
> *have fallen asleep. Then he appeared to James, then to*
> *all the apostles, and last of all he appeared to me also, as*
> *to one abnormally born.* (1 Corinthians 15:3–7)

There have been those like Frank Morrison—an inves-
tigative journalist who started out as a rank sceptic—who
looked into the story of the Resurrection, and under the
impact of the facts became a convinced believer in the testimony of Scripture. His book, *Who Moved The Stone?*, is an
eloquent witness to the historical fact of the physical resurrection of Jesus from the dead.

b. A spiritual reality

Having said all that, it is not only the obvious and outward
facts which give the Resurrection its power and relevance as
far as God or the Christian is concerned. The important
truths are the deep and profound spiritual truths that are
involved in the Resurrection.

For example, when Paul writes to the Romans, he highlights the fact that the raising of Jesus from the dead was a
tremendous affirmation on the part of God as to who Jesus
really is.

> *who through the Spirit of holiness was declared with*
> *power to be the Son of God by his resurrection from the*
> *dead: Jesus Christ our Lord.* (Romans 1:4)

In the Resurrection, God the Father, is giving His Amen to all that has been accomplished in the life and death of Jesus. Again, the Resurrection *out of the tomb* is not seen as significant in itself. It is the fact that Jesus is raised far above all the heavens to the place of absolute authority which is most important. Time and again the New Testament writers stress this point. No one better than Paul, in Philippians 2:

> *Therefore God exalted him to the highest place and gave him the name that is above every name, that at the name of Jesus every knee should bow, in heaven and on earth and under the earth, and every tongue confess that Jesus Christ is Lord, to the glory of God the Father.*
>
> (Philippians 2:9–11)

These words have been identified, by some commentators, as a hymn or confession commonly used in the early Church. If this be true, it only serves to strengthen the conviction of these early believers of the spiritual significance of the Resurrection of Jesus. The same thought is echoed powerfully in the vision of John in the book of Revelation:

> *I am the Living One; I was dead, and behold I am alive for ever and ever! And I hold the keys of death and Hades.*
> (Revelation 1:18)

These last words show us the point of this. We have already seen that the Cross is the climactic battle between God and Satan. The powers of darkness met their match in the peerless power of the Son of Man.

The skirmishes continue on the earth, but the decisive victory has been won and now Jesus Christ reigns in power. The Father has declared to the Son:

Sit at my right hand until I make your enemies a footstool for your feet. (Hebrews 1:13)

The New Testament gives us an insight into the present activity of the Son of God on behalf of every Christian believer. The Epistle to the Hebrews stresses this outcome of the Ascension for us:

because Jesus lives forever, he has a permanent priest-hood. Therefore he is able to save completely those who come to God through him, because he always lives to intercede for them. (Hebrews 7:24,25)

The power of that is underlined by Paul when he speaks of this intercession in the context of our security in Christ.

Who is he that condemns? Christ Jesus, who died—more than that, who was raised to life—is at the right hand of God and is also interceding for us. Who shall separate us from the love of Christ? (Romans 8:34,35)

c. A personal experience

The New Testament is at pains to show that all the proceeds of the Cross are made good in our lives because of the power of the Resurrection. If James had not risen from the dead, then none of our salvation or victory would have been secure. Without the Resurrection, we would worship a dead martyr like many other religions do.

Jesus is no dead hero, however, but a living Saviour and the ascended Lord. He was raised from the dead by the power of the Holy Spirit and He now sends forth the same Spirit into our lives to make real all those things He has achieved and won for us through His Death.

It is part of the present work of the Holy Spirit to take

that which has been worked in and through Jesus and make it real in those who respond to Him in faith. Just as Jesus died to sin, so in the Spirit I can die to the power of sin (Romans 6:5). Just as Jesus broke the power of evil in His body through His suffering, so that evil power is overcome in me by the same Spirit (1 John 4:4).

We can consider some of the benefits of the Resurrection which the Holy Spirit makes real in us by His living indwelling power.

—Spiritual Life—Jesus told His disciples that because he lived, we would live also (John 14:19). And that is the truth. Just as the Holy Spirit breathed the life of God into Jesus and brought Him out of death, so the Spirit breathes into us and imparts the life of God into the very centre of our being.

—Victory over sin—It was the principle and power of sin in all its aspects which Jesus dealt with on the Cross. Death, fear, bondage, oppression, disobedience, despair, uncertainty and so on are the effects of sin in our lives. Sin is not a theory, but a real power. Sin becomes a personal force expressing itself through the psychological and spiritual powers which dominate our minds and actions. Every man since Adam has been pulled down by that negative influence and, in the end, it has issued in death. Jesus, however, was different. Having taken sin upon Himself and gone through the process right into death, He broke through and out of the clutches of sin and its power into the liberty of resurrection life. It is that very process of redemption which the Holy Spirit makes real in you and me through faith.

If, by the trespass of the one man, death reigned through that one man, how much more will those who receive God's abundant provision of grace and of the gift of righteousness reign in life through the one man, Jesus Christ. (Romans 5:17)

Spiritual Power—Two great New Testament Greek words spell out the extent of the power of God which is made available to us in a personal way as a result of the Resurrection of Jesus. The Risen Jesus lives and acts in this power Himself and through His Spirit He shares it into our lives.

The first is *exousia*, which is the power of being. It is a word that is normally translated 'authority'. it carries within it the idea of 'having the right to'. It is the sort of word that would be appropriate to an ambassador who represents his country in another land. He himself may not be a very significant person, but he has power! He has the authority of his whole government and country at home behind him. So with us, the Holy Spirit confirms our relationship with God through faith in Jesus and into our hearts he spreads the confidence or certainty of who we really are in Christ (see John 1:12, Romans 8:16 and 1 John 3:1).

The second is *dunamis*, which is the power of doing. It is an active word. it carries the idea of ability and motive power within itself. It sounds quite like 'dynamite' and, in fact, that is sometimes what it looks like when God acts. Jesus said to His disciples:

> *You will receive power when the Holy Spirit comes on you, and you will be my witnesses in Jerusalem and in all Judea and Samaria, and to the ends of the earth.*
>
> (Acts 1:8)

Peter says the same:

> *His divine power has given us everything we need for life and godliness through our knowledge of him who called us by his own glory and goodness.* (2 Peter 1:3)

—Spiritual Gifts and Ministries—The operation of the gifts of the Holy Spirit within the Body of Christ are an important witness to the fact of the Ascension. Paul makes this clear when he discusses the gifts of leadership and ministry within the Church. He connects their operation on earth directly with the ministry of the Risen and Ascended Lord in Glory.

> *(He who descended is the very one who ascended higher than all the heavens, in order to fill the whole universe.) It was he who gave some to be apostles, some to be prophets, some to be evangelists, and some to be pastors and teachers.* (Ephesians 4:10,11)

—The Hope of Glory— God is a God of hope and we participate in His hope through the inner work of the Holy Spirit. The ground of our hope, however, is that substantive work which God achieved in raising Jesus from the dead. It is the door of glory. We must understand that hope in the Scriptures doesn't mean 'hopefulness'. It is not wishful thinking. It is a deep, personal experience of the eternal confidence of God. He has begun His work and He will finish it, and the Resurrection of Jesus is the outstanding testimony to that fact!

> *Praise be to the God and Father of our Lord Jesus Christ! In his great mercy he has given us new birth into a living hope through the resurrection of Jesus Christ from the dead, and into an inheritance that can never perish, spoil or fade—kept in heaven for you.* (1 Peter 1:3,4)

We could go on and on exploring the benefits of the Cross and Resurrection which the Spirit makes real in us through faith. Look through the Scriptures yourself and grasp the promise!

d. A future promise

The Resurrection fulfils one last important function we need to consider briefly. *It stands as an interim statement of an as yet uncompleted work!*

The Cross was not only a day of victory, it was a day of judgement. It was a day when God passed judgement on sin and all its outcome, but He also passed judgement on the devil,

> *the ruler of the kingdom of the air, the spirit who is now at work in those who are disobedient.* (Ephesians 2:2)

Some of the last words Jesus said to His disciples underline the same point:

> *Now is the time for judgment on this world, now the prince of this world will be driven out.* (John 12:31)

Here is the fulfilment of that prophetic word of God to the serpent recorded in Genesis 3:15:

> *He will crush your head, and you will strike his heel.*

The judgement effected that day is still being carried out and will be brought to its final conclusion on God's Great Day. It is the act of the Resurrection in power that ties the judgement that has been passed with the judgement yet to come. The Resurrection of Jesus stands like a signal to remind men and the devil, lest they forget, to whom the last word really does belong! This was the heart of what Paul proclaimed in heathen Athens:

> *In the past God overlooked such ignorance, but now he commands all people everywhere to repent. For he has set a day when he will judge the world with justice by the*

man he has appointed. He has given proof of this to all
men by raising him from the dead. (Acts 17:30,31)

The very same sign that is a warning to unbelief is, of
course, the source of great joy and anticipation for faith.

Dear friends, now we are children of God, and what we
will be has not yet been made known. But we know that
when he appears, we shall be like him, for we shall see
him as he is. Everyone who has this hope in him purifies
himself, just as he is pure. (1 John 3:2,3)

Give me a sight, O Saviour,
Of Thy wondrous love to me;
Of the love that brought Thee down to earth,
To die on Calvary.

O wonder of all wonders,
That thro' Thy death for me,
My open sins, my secret sins,
Can all forgiven be.
Then melt my heart, O Saviour,
Bend me, yea, break me down,
Until I own Thee Conqueror,
And Lord and Sov'reign crown.

Katherine A.M. Kelly